Voltaire

THE PROFILES IN LITERATURE SERIES

GENERAL EDITOR : B. C. SOUTHAM, M.A., B.LITT. (OXON.)
*Formerly Department of English, Westfield College,
University of London*

Volumes in this series include

CHARLOTTE BRONTË	Arthur Pollard
EMILY AND ANNE BRONTË	W. H. Stevenson
CHARLES DICKENS	Martin Fido
GEORGE ELIOT	Ian Adam
WILLIAM FAULKNER	Eric Mottram
HENRY FIELDING	C. J. Rawson
ELIZABETH GASKELL	John McVeagh
NATHANIEL HAWTHORNE	J. Donald Crowley
JAMES JOYCE	Arnold Goldman
D. H. LAWRENCE	R. P. Draper
HERMAN MELVILLE	D. E. S. Maxwell
THOMAS LOVE PEACOCK	Carl Dawson
SAMUEL RICHARDSON	A. M. Kearney
WALTER SCOTT	Robin Mayhead
JONATHAN SWIFT	Kathleen Williams
TOLSTOY	Ronald Hayman
ANTHONY TROLLOPE	P. D. Edwards
MARK TWAIN	I. M. Walker
W. B. YEATS	N. Jeffares
EMILE ZOLA	Philip Walker

Voltaire

by Christopher Thacker

Lecturer in French,
University of Reading

LONDON
ROUTLEDGE & KEGAN PAUL

First published 1971
by Routledge & Kegan Paul Limited
Broadway House, 68-74 Carter Lane
London EC4V 5EL
Printed in Great Britain
by Northumberland Press Ltd
Gateshead
© Christopher Thacker 1971
ISBN 0 7100 7020 9 (C)

The Profiles in Literature Series

This series is designed to provide the student of literature and the general reader with a brief and helpful introduction to the major novelists and prose writers in English, American and foreign literature.

Each volume will provide an account of an individual author's writing career and works, through a series of carefully chosen extracts illustrating the major aspects of the author's art. These extracts are accompanied by commentary and analysis, drawing attention to particular features of the style and treatment. There is no pretence, of course, that a study of extracts can give a sense of the works as a whole, but this selective approach enables the reader to focus his attention upon specific features, and to be informed in his approach by experienced critics and scholars who are contributing to the series.

The volumes will provide a particularly helpful and practical form of introduction to writers whose works are extensive or which present special problems for the modern reader, who can then proceed with a sense of his bearings and an informed eye for the writer's art.

An important feature of these books is the extensive reference list of the author's works and the descriptive list of the most useful biographies, commentaries and critical studies.

B.C.S.

Contents

CONTENTS

Voltaire: his life and works

Candide—'the only sort of novel you can really read'. Frederick the Great said this in 1759, the year *Candide* was published. Since then the world has read many novels, and many great ones; but Voltaire's *Candide* remains one of the very best, probably the most famous book in the whole of French literature. It is one of the rare works whose subject (and the treatment of it!) seems always close to our own times, and our own affairs. Voltaire writes about the world, what happens in it, and what happens to the men and women—yourself, myself, our family, neighbours, strangers, friends and enemies—who swarm upon its surface.

Famous though *Candide* is, surprisingly few people read much further in Voltaire's immense, varied and fascinating writings. Yet Voltaire is not a man of a 'single book', but the writer of a hundred, and more, a giant among the giants of literature.

Goethe, a giant himself, thought highly of Voltaire. Listing Voltaire's merits in his commentary on Diderot's *Neveu de Rameau*, he poured out this list of qualities: 'Profundity, genius, intuition, greatness, spontaneity, talent, merit, nobility, imagination, wit, understanding, feeling, sensibility, taste, good taste, rightness, propriety, tone, good tone, courtliness, variety, abundance, wealth, fecundity, warmth, magic, charm, grace, urbanity, facility, vivacity, fineness, brilliance, boldness, sparkle, mordancy, delicacy, ingenuity, style, versification, harmony, purity, correctness, elegance, perfection.' We might think this was sufficient—but Goethe went on to complete his account by claiming Voltaire as the 'greatest writer of all time' and 'the most astounding creation of the author of nature'.

Though we need not rate Voltaire quite so superlatively, he is still one of France's greatest writers, and during his long life—1694-1778—his prolific literary creations included major works in every known genre, in verse, in prose, fiction and non-fiction, short poems, odes, epic poems, dialogues, tragedies, comedies, stories, novels, works of philosophy, historical works, scores of pamphlets, tracts, brochures and essays on literary, scientific, religious, political and personal subjects, and (if this was not enough!) thousands of letters—of which some 20,000 have survived.

His life, interests and activities cover most of the eighteenth century, and his connections in time extend far back into the seventeenth and a good way on into the nineteenth. In his *Age of Louis XIV*, he speaks of meeting people who had been at Dover in 1660, to witness the return of King Charles II of England when he came back from exile. Before Voltaire's death in 1778, many people had been born who were to be famous in the nineteenth century—Chateaubriand, Constant, Mme de Staël, Napoleon, Wordsworth, Scott, Goethe, Beethoven.

Born in Paris, he was given the Christian names François-Marie, and until 1718 he was known by his father's surname, Arouet. His father, a lawyer, tried to make him become a lawyer too, but François-Marie preferred poetry, the company of elegant and intelligent patrons, and the

2

prospect of a life lived in and near the French court. In 1716, a satirical poem earned him his first period in exile. It was not painful—he spent the time at the mansion of a nobleman—but exiles were to recur through most of his life: he wrote witty, profound and penetrating, often malicious pieces which brought him immense applause, and which simultaneously created embittered enemies. As his skill and fame increased, the applause was justly greater—few writers have been so famous for so large a part of their lifetime as Voltaire—but his enemies drove him into longer and more complete forms of exile. He was rarely content to accept these reverses, but fought back ferociously. His personal satires became a terrible weapon, admired by those who were not involved, feared and hated by the victims.

Œdipe, the first of many plays, was performed in 1718, and was an immense success. Aged twenty-four, he was hailed as France's greatest living dramatist, the worthy successor to Corneille and Racine. He changed his name to Voltaire—probably an anagram on AROVET L*e I*eune, or 'Arouet junior'—and took for himself the prefix 'de', the prerogative of a gentleman. In 1723 his epic poem the *Henriade* appeared, bringing him as great a fame as an epic poet as *Œdipe* had brought him as a dramatist. In 1726, after a quarrel with a nobleman, he was sent to the Bastille, and soon after exiled to England, where he spent two years. His political and religious sympathies were crystallized by the differences which he found between English and French attitudes, and expressed in the *Lettres philosophiques* (or *Letters Concerning the English Nation*), published in 1733. This work is one of the earliest yet most sweeping attacks to be made on the French system, the *ancien régime*, before the Revolution.

Meanwhile he had become famous as a historian. His-torical writings were, with the theatre, to be the work he

3

undertook most seriously. His works, such as the *Age of Louis XIV* and the *Essay on Universal History (Essai sur les mœurs)*, cover the entire history of civilization, and mark the beginning of modern historical writing.

In the 1730s Voltaire began two vital friendships. The first was in 1733 with Mme du Châtelet, an intellectual and an aristocrat who became his mistress. Then in 1736 Frederick, Crown Prince of Prussia (the future Frederick II, or Frederick the Great) wrote a long letter of praise and philosophical interest to Voltaire. The correspondence flattered both sides—Voltaire was delighted to be approached by so eminent a nobleman, Frederick was passionately enthusiastic about French culture, and wanted the friendship of France's foremost author. When Mme du Châtelet died in 1749, Frederick (now King of Prussia) persuaded Voltaire to join his cosmopolitan circle of intellectuals at Potsdam, near Berlin, and from 1750 to 1753 Voltaire was attached to Frederick's court.

Voltaire and Frederick quarrelled, and Voltaire's retreat —or escape—from Potsdam in 1753 was followed by a humiliating detention at Frankfurt. The royal patron had been an intolerant friend. Voltaire's resentment led to his writing, in 1758-9, the savage *Memoirs of M. de Voltaire*, in which Frederick's life and his bitter-sweet friendship with Voltaire are drawn with cruel, brilliant strokes.

In the late 1750s, Voltaire struggled to establish his personal freedom. He found safety in Switzerland, first at Lausanne, then at Geneva, and then in 1759 at Ferney in France, just across the border from Geneva.

The idea of personal independence, of winning some kind of freedom from the oppression of governments and autocratic institutions such as the Church, is a strong theme both in the *Memoirs* and in Voltaire's most famous work, the novel *Candide*, published in 1759. Since the early 1740s Voltaire had taken to writing *contes* or 'short stories', and

Candide is both the best of these, and one of the longest, long enough at least for it to be called a 'novel'.

In most of Voltaire's *contes* the hero is a traveller, who observes, experiences, suffers sometimes, in many parts of the world. In the smaller and less ambitious *contes*, there is usually one straightforward 'philosophic' message which is revealed in the hero's travels, of a social, political or religious nature, but *Candide*, though splendidly single-minded in its exposure of the world's evils, has a dazzling complexity of allusion which makes it one of the richest of all Voltaire's works. It has been suggested that the heroes of the various *contes*, travelling, seeing, experiencing as they do, are representative of Voltaire himself, telling us a great deal of his changing feelings both about himself and about society and mankind in general. Certainly *Candide*, written when he was well over sixty, sums up the interests of a lifetime, and the culmination of his concern at the sad, vicious muddle the world is in.

From the time of *Candide*, and from the time of his settling in and near Geneva, in 1758-9, Voltaire's satire and indignation, though no less vociferous, are given a *practical* application which they had not received so fully before. At Ferney Voltaire flung himself whole-heartedly into the task of improving the conditions of the peasants and artisans who lived on and near his estate. He took up the case of the peasants who, at the nearby abbey of Saint-Claude, were still legally bound as serfs belonging to the abbey. And, most famous of the causes which he took up, he defended the Calas family, Protestant victims of Catholic persecution. Again, fearing that the great *Encyclopédie*, written by the combined *philosophes* or liberal free-thinkers in the 1750s and 1760s, was too ponderous to have a proper reforming and enlightening effect, he wrote his own 'portable encyclopædia', the *Philosophical Dictionary* (1764). Later, in the 1770s, alarmed that the extremists among the *philosophes* were earning his cause the reputation of irreligion, he launched a campaign attacking the concept of atheism. Finally in 1778 he returned from Ferney to Paris, the champion of the oppressed, and the greatest writer of the age. He was eighty-three. The tumultuous welcome, the endless activities and excitements in which he continued to involve himself, all conspired to exhaust him. Within four months of his return to Paris, he was dead.

Voltaire's significance today

Macaulay, disturbed by the relentless, lethal ferocity of Voltaire's attacks on individuals, on institutions, on general failings such as hypocrisy or intolerance, saw Voltaire as a purely negative spirit, which he outlined in his essay 'Frederick the Great' in these splendid, admiring and yet critical phrases: 'Voltaire could not build: he could only pull down: he was the very Vitruvius of ruin. He has bequeathed to us not a single doctrine to be called by his name, not a single addition to the stock of our positive knowledge.'

Certainly Voltaire was the great demolisher of the eighteenth century, exposing, unmasking, piercing, tearing down, *destroying* the multiple and fearsome forms of complacency, humbug and horror which he found. But just as surely Voltaire was a positive spirit of rare energy and intelligence. Through his work we see a mighty champion in the cause of peace, tolerance, justice, freedom—and sanity. Certainly he attacked the 'glory' and the 'heroism' of war, the pretensions to absolute power of kings and institutions, the persecutions carried out in the name of religion—but these were, and are, realities which no honest person can deny. Now as I write civilians are massacred in Cambodia, a terrible war destroys both sides in Vietnam, and an earthquake shatters countless homes in Turkey, while grotesque accidents and cruel disease maim and torture those around us every day. Voltaire could not close his eyes to this truth. Then, as now, terrible things were happening, happening to human beings. As Arthur Miller puts it in *Death of a Salesman*, 'So attention must be paid'.

The clarity, the humour, the compassion with which Voltaire invites us to 'pay attention', the humane and noble principles which he would have us respect, the good sense and thoughtfulness of his observations—these are all eminently constructive. Though the particular form of an injustice may have disappeared, the general nature of complacency, humbug and fanaticism reappears in every age, and can only be fought by those same general principles of justice, tolerance and sanity which are so lucidly put forward in his writings.

Voltaire's prose style is superbly suited to his thought. Confusion, vagueness, false mystery, pomposity are absent, and clarity, proportion and directness prevail. Generally, the sentences are short, tidy, without obscurity, though this does not mean for a moment that they lack art. Even when he is presenting something ridiculous and false, such as the philosophy of Pangloss, in *Candide*, this demonstration is clear and balanced, with a ludicrous yet understandable opening, 'It is demonstrable ... that things cannot be otherwise than as they are ...' followed by a crystal-clear list of the ridiculous proofs of this theory, and concluded by a triumphantly lucid reaffirmation of this crass belief : 'They who assert, that every thing is right, do not express themselves correctly; they should say that every thing is for the best.'

Denying the possibility of metaphysical enquiry, Voltaire guides his sympathies and thought to shed a brilliant light on the problems of the actual world. *Mankind* is his subject —and *reason* is the special prerogative of man's mind. Voltaire's prose reflects the trust of the eighteenth-century *philosophes* in the value of reason. If our thought runs clear, unmuddied by prejudice, superstition or fanaticism, then our language must reflect this clarity. In the century of the Enlightenment, none wrote more clearly than Voltaire.

Scheme of extracts

The title-list of Voltaire's works would fill half this book. The *Complete Works of Voltaire* now being published under the supervision of Dr Theodore Besterman is to include at least 136 volumes of some 300 pages apiece. Compression and ruthless elimination are both essential if Voltaire is to be introduced with a selection of his work in a hundred or so pages.

I have chosen seven major topics from his work, within which the extracts are numbered consecutively, so that cross-references can help to increase the reader's understanding. The topics are arranged in roughly chronological order, beginning with Voltaire's writings about England, dating from the 1730s, and ending with his writings in defence of the oppressed, dating from the 1760s onwards.

There is, unavoidably, a certain overlapping. For example, during the final period of his humanitarian activity, his earlier interests in literary and historical matters were as keen as ever. Again, his continuing interest in a subject may lead to his treating it in different ways at different times. At the risk of an over-narrow selection I have occasionally tried to emphasize this—including, for example, a historical passage on the Inquisition (13) together with a fictional presentation of the same thing (22).

The translations are taken mainly from eighteenth-century English editions. Though most of these are available only through libraries, they have a flavour which helps to give something of the feeling of Voltaire's eighteenth-century French. Modern English translations are listed in the select bibliography at the end of the book.

England

'You know England: are they as great fools in that country as in France?' *Candide*, Ch. xxiii.

Voltaire, exiled in England for most of the period 1726-8, and smarting under a sense of injustice, was quick to seize upon the differences between French and English society. His *Letters Concerning the English Nation* were probably sketched out in 1728 or 1729, though they were not published until 1733 (in English) and 1734 (in French).

In this book, the unifying theme is the insistence on the different ways in which the English enjoy a *freedom* which, implicitly, is lacking in France, and the emphasis on the benefits which this freedom brings. Voltaire certainly exaggerated at times, or chose to ignore, disadvantages (such as the inferior status of Roman Catholics) which would weaken his case. But the vast majority of his points had a great deal of truth, and revealed to the French more forcibly than any previous book the defects and injustices of their own system.

Voltaire's survey is broad and deep—no simple guidebook, this, but a thorough, profound examination of the entire society. He learnt English with remarkable speed and completeness, and made a great number of varied acquaintances. He had already met Lord Bolingbroke in France in 1720, and quickly acquired introductions to many of the most eminent people of the time, Lord Peterborough, Walpole, Pope, Swift, Gay, Thomson, Young, Clarke and Berkeley. He read widely—theology, literature, scientific, philosophical, historical and political writings—and his insatiable curiosity led him to find out for himself about many specialities of English life—trade, the Stock Exchange, the theatre, and the different sects which religious toleration allowed to exist in England. Liberty, toleration: the words echo through the book, and lie at the very centre of Voltaire's way of thought. 'An Englishman,' he writes in Letter 5, 'as one to whom liberty is natural, may go to heaven his own way.'

1   The Quakers (Letter 1)

This sect, discussed in the first four letters, deserves its prominence for two main reasons—there was no equivalent sect whatsoever in the Catholic-dominated France he wished to enlighten: and he felt that the reasoned simplicity of the Quakers' belief came nearer than any other form of Christianity to his own deist views. The two following passages show Voltaire's skill in making one side of an argument look absurd, and thus giving strength to the other. The Frenchman's questions are made to appear hasty and thoughtless, and victory celebrations are shown as a heartless mockery.

The Quaker was a hale ruddy complexion'd old man, who had never been afflicted with sickness, because he had always been insensible to passions, and a perfect stranger to intemperance. I never in my life saw a more noble or a more engaging aspect than his.

After taking part of a frugal meal, which began and ended with a prayer to God, I began to question my courteous host. I open'd with that which good Catholicks have more than once made to Huguenots. 'My dear sir, says I, were you ever baptiz'd?—I never was, replied the Quaker, nor any of my brethren.—Zouns, says I to him, you are not Christians then.—Friend, replies the old man in a soft tone of voice, swear not; we are Christians, and endeavour to be good Christians, but we are not of opinion, that the sprinkling water on a child's head makes him a Christian.— Heavens! says I, shock'd at his impiety, you have then forgot that *Christ* was baptiz'd by St. *John*.—Friend, replies the mild Quaker once again, swear not. *Christ* indeed was baptiz'd by *John*, but he himself never baptiz'd any one. We are the disciples of *Christ*, not *John*.'

(Cf. 24, 34)

'We never war or fight in any case; but 'tis not that we are afraid, for so far from shuddering at the thoughts of death, we on the contrary bless the moment which unites us with the Being of Beings; but the reason of our not using the outward sword is, that we are neither wolves, tygers, nor mastiffs, but men and Christians. Our God, who has commanded us to love our enemies, and to suffer without repining, would certainly not permit us to cross the seas, merely because murtherers cloath'd in scarlet, and wearing caps two foot high enlist citizens by a noise made with two little sticks on an ass's skin extended. And when, after a victory is gain'd, the whole city of *London* is illuminated; when the sky is in a blaze with fireworks, and a noise is heard in the air of thanksgivings, of bells, of organs, and of the cannon, we groan in silence, and are deeply affected with sadness of spirit and brokenness of heart, for the sad havock which is the occasion of those public rejoycings.'

(Cf. 21)

2   *Trade: an advantage of religious toleration* (Letter 6)
French readers would see in this passage an allusion to the
lack of toleration in France, and especially to the revocation of the Edict of Nantes in 1685, which had guaranteed
religious freedom to the French Protestants, the Huguenots.
Because of the revocation, some 200,000 Huguenots had
left France, a serious loss of skilled and productive workers.
Many had emigrated to England.

Take a view of the *Royal-Exchange* in *London*, a place
more venerable than many courts of justice, where the
representatives of all nations meet for the benefit of mankind. There the Jew, the Mahometan, and the Christian
transact together as tho' they all profess'd the same religion,
and give the name of Infidel to none but bankrupts. There
the Presbyterian confides in the Anabaptist, and the Church-
man depends on the Quaker's word. At the breaking up of
this pacific and free assembly, some withdraw to the
synagogue, and others to take a glass. This man goes and is
baptiz'd in a great tub, in the name of the Father, Son, and
Holy Ghost: That man has his son's foreskin cut off,
whilst a sett of *Hebrew* words (quite unintelligible to him)
are mumbled over his child. Others retire to their churches,
and there wait for the inspiration of heaven with their
hats on, and all are satisfied.
   If one religion only were allowed in *England*, the government would very possibly become arbitrary; if there
were but two, the people wou'd cut one another's throats;
but as there are such a multitude, they all live happily
and in peace.

(Cf. 42)

3   *Trade: the strength of a free nation* (Letter 10)

Voltaire saw clearly how England's prosperity was a
genuine part of her strength, and how France suffered by
the refusal of the ruling nobility to engage in trade. Again,

'freedom' is a key word.

As Trade enrich'd the Citizens in *England*, so it contributed to their Freedom, and this Freedom on the other Side
extended their Commerce, whence arose the Grandeur of
the State.... Posterity will very possibly be surpriz'd to
hear that an Island whose only Produce is a little Lead, Tin,
Fuller's Earth, and coarse Wool, should become so powerful by its Commerce, as to be able to send in 1723, three
Fleets at the same Time to three different and far distanc'd
Parts of the Globe.... Such a Circumstance as this raises a
just Pride in an *English* Merchant, and makes him presume
(not without some Reason) to compare himself to a *Roman*
Citizen; and indeed a Peer's Brother does not think Traffic
beneath him. When the Lord *Townshend* was Minister of
State, a Brother of his was content to be a City Merchant;
and at the Time that the Earl of *Oxford* govern'd *Great-
Britain*, his younger Brother was no more than a Factor
in *Aleppo*, where he chose to live, and where he died.

In *France* the Title of Marquis is given *gratis* to any one
who will accept of it; and whosoever arrives at *Paris*
from the midst of the most remote Provinces with Money
in his Purse, and a Name terminating in *ac* or *ille*, may
strut about, and cry, such a Man as I! A Man of my Rank
and Figure! And may look down upon a Trader with
sovereign Contempt; whilst the Trader on the other Side,
by thus often hearing his Profession treated so disdainfully,
is Fool enough to blush at it. However, I need not say
which is most useful to a Nation; a Lord, powder'd in the
tip of the Mode, who knows exactly at what a Clock the
King rises and goes to bed; and who gives himself Airs of
Grandeur and State, at the same Time that he is acting the
Slave in the Anti-chamber of a prime Minister; or a Merchant, who enriches his Country, dispatches Orders from
his Compting-House to *Surat* and *Grand Cairo*, and con-
tributes to the Felicity of the World.

4 *The fruit of civil war: a constitutional monarchy*
(Letter 8)

Unlike the religious and civil wars in France, which had led to an autocratic monarchy and a single religion, the civil wars in England had led both to religious and to political freedom.

The *English* are the only people upon earth who have been able to prescribe limits to the power of Kings by resisting them; and who, by a series of struggles, have at last establish'd that wise Government, where the Prince is all powerful to do good, and at the same time is restrain'd from committing evil; where the Nobles are great without insolence, tho' there are no Vassals; and where the People share in the government without confusion.... The *English* have doubtless purchas'd their Liberties at a very high price, and waded thro' seas of blood to drown the Idol of arbitrary Power. Other nations have been involv'd in as great calamities, and have shed as much blood; but then the blood they spilt in defence of their Liberties, only enslaved them the more.

5 *One justice for all: and fair taxation* (Letter 9)

While the different classes in France—nobility, clergy, bourgeoisie and peasants—were each subject to separate laws, privileges and systems of taxation, in which the nobility and the clergy were often granted freedoms denied to others, and could obtain exemption from taxes which poorer people had to pay, such injustices had been abolished in England.

There is no such thing here, as *haute, moyenne, & basse* justice, that is, a Power to judge in all Matters civil and criminal; nor a Right or Privilege of Hunting in the Grounds of a Citizen, who at the same time is not permitted to fire a Gun in his own Field.

No one is exempted in this Country from paying certain Taxes, because he is a Nobleman or a Priest. All Duties and Taxes are settled by the House of Commons, whose Power is greater than that of the Peers, tho' inferiour to it in dignity. The spiritual as well as temporal Lords have the Liberty to reject a Money Bill brought in by the Commons, but they are not allow'd to alter any thing in it, and must either pass or throw it out without Restriction. When the Bill has passed the Lords and is sign'd by the King, then the whole Nation pays, every Man in proportion to his Revenue or Estate, not according to his Title, which would be absurd. There is no such thing as an arbitrary Subsidy or Poll-Tax, but a real Tax on the Lands, of all which an Estimate was made in the Reign of the famous King *William* the Third.

The Land-Tax continues still upon the same foot, tho' the Revenue of the Lands is increas'd. Thus no one is tyranniz'd over, and every one is easy. The Feet of the Peasants are not bruis'd by wooden Shoes; they eat white Bread, are well cloath'd, and are not afraid of increasing their Stock of Cattle, nor of tiling their Houses, from any Apprehensions that their Taxes will be rais'd the Year following. The annual Income of the Estates of a great many Commoners in *England*, amounts to two hundred thousand Livres; and yet these don't think it beneath them to plough the Lands which enrich them, and on which they enjoy their Liberty.

(Cf. 41)

6 *Locke: the down-to-earth philosopher* (Letter 13)

Voltaire admired the practical attitude of the English philosopher, who examined human affairs without assuming any metaphysical truths beforehand. Locke, Voltaire claimed, was too modest to assert any absolute knowledge of the unknowable. Let us concentrate our feeble human powers on the world around us, and explore what we know through our senses to exist.

Such a Multitude of Reasoners having written the Romance of the Soul, a Sage at last arose, who gave, with an Air of the greatest Modesty, the History of it. Mr. *Locke* has display'd the human Soul, in the same Manner as an excellent Anatomist explains the Springs of the human Body. He every where takes the Light of Physicks for his Guide. He sometimes presumes to speak affirmatively, but then he presumes also to doubt. Instead of concluding at once what we know not, he examines gradually what we wou'd know. He takes an Infant at the Instant of his Birth; he traces, Step by Step, the Progress of his Understanding; examines what Things he has in common with Beasts, and what he possesses above them. Above all he consults himself; the being conscious that he himself thinks. . . . Mr. *Locke* after having laid down, from the most solid Principles, that Ideas enter the Mind through the Senses; having examin'd our simple and complex Ideas; having trac'd the human Mind through its several Operations; having shew'd that all the Languages in the World are imperfect, and the great Abuse that is made of Words every Moment; he at last comes to consider the Extent or rather the narrow Limits of human Knowledge. 'Twas in this Chapter he presum'd to advance, but very modestly, the following Words, 'We shall, perhaps, never be capable of knowing, whether a Being, purely material, thinks or not.'

If I might presume to give my Opinion on so delicate a Subject after Mr. *Locke*, I would say, that Men have long disputed on the Nature and the Immortality of the Soul. With regard to its Immortality, 'tis impossible to give a Demonstration of it, since its Nature is still the Subject of Controversy; which however must be thoroughly understood, before a Person can be able to determine whether it be immortal or not. Human Reason is so little able, merely by its own Strength, to demonstrate the Immortality of the Soul, that 'twas absolutely necessary Religion should reveal it to us.

(Cf. 36)

7 *Merit duly honoured* (Letter 23)

Voltaire was in England when Newton died, and witnessed his honourable funeral. He wanted Frenchmen to think of their own neglect, or even their rejection, of great thinkers such as Descartes or Bayle, and also to reflect on the inhuman way actors and actresses were treated by the Church in France on their death. Adrienne Lecouvreur, the most famous French actress of her day, was refused Christian burial when she died in 1730.

Sir *Isaac Newton* was rever'd in his Life-time, and had a due respect paid to him after his Death; the greatest Men in the Nation disputing who shou'd have the Honour of holding up his Pall. Go into *Westminster-Abbey*, and you'll find that what raises the Admiration of the Spectator is not the Mausoleums of the *English* Kings, but the Monuments which the Gratitude of the Nation has erected, to perpetuate the Memory of those illustrious Men who contributed to its Glory. We view their Statues in that Abbey in the same Manner, as those of *Sophocles, Plato* and other immortal Personages were view'd in *Athens*; and I am persuaded, that the bare Sight of those glorious Monuments has fir'd more than one Breast, and been the Occasion of their becoming great Men.

The *English* have even been reproach'd with paying too extravagant Honours to mere Merit, and censured for interring the celebrated Actress Mrs. *Oldfield* in *Westminster-Abbey*, with almost the same Pomp as Sir *Isaac Newton*. Some pretend that the *English* had paid her these great Funeral Honours, purposely to make us more strongly sensible of the Barbarity and Injustice which they object to us, for having buried *Mademoiselle Lecouvreur* ignominiously in the Fields.

(Cf. 12)

The great writer

'You must be new, without being odd, often sublime but always natural; you must know the human heart and make it speak.' *Candide*, Ch. xxii.

In his major 'public' works—epic poetry, tragedy and history—Voltaire writes with assurance as the leader of the leading culture in Europe. Generally speaking, the Enlightenment, and Voltaire as one of its principal spokesmen, was confident in its sense of superiority over the past, and in its hope to succeed eventually in creating a new and more humane society. Though not all *philosophes* wished for radical change, they certainly sought improvement, the reform of what was bad, and literature in their hands served these humane, rational and practical aims. Literature was a searchlight, revealing the best, stating the truth, unmasking what was false and corrupt. The writer is seen as one of the noblest products of the age, his works as the quintessence of what the men of the age have thought, the burnished mirror of men and society.

Though Voltaire wrote in virtually every known genre, and developed others such as the *conte* (see chapter on

'*Candide*') and the philosophical dialogue which had not known much fame before, he believed all his life that only the traditionally great genres—epic poetry and tragedy—together with history in prose, were really deserving of a writer's serious attention. Ironically, his productions in the first two categories, though immensely applauded in his lifetime, were so closely linked to the models and precepts of previous masters—the example of Virgil's *Aeneid*, and the tragedies of Corneille and Racine—that his own originality was restricted, and these works of Voltaire's are no longer much appreciated.

The limits prescribed for the form and content of historical writing were much less rigid, and here Voltaire's genius was able to develop more effectively. In the best of his historical works, the *Essay on Universal History* (*Essai sur les mœurs*), and the *Age of Louis XIV*, his sustained grasp of the total, complex picture of events and his choice of accurate, telling detail make him the first truly modern historian.

8   *Epic: the Grand Manner*

The *Henriade* (first published in 1723) tells the story of Henri IV's success in unifying the French, towards the end of the sixteenth century. For Voltaire, Henri IV was in many ways the founder of the nation, as Virgil's Aeneas represented the founder of Rome. The opening lines are consciously Virgilian:

I sing the Hero, who by Right of Arms,
And Right of Royal Heirship reign'd in *France*,
Who by long Labours learn'd to rule, who knew
Mighty and Mild, to conquer and forgive,
Who *Mayne*, the *League* and proud *Iberia* tam'd,
Conq'ror and Father of his Country, He.

(*Henriade*, I, ll. 1-6)

9 Poetry: the Grand Manner on a smaller scale

Voltaire's poetic output runs to tens of thousands of lines. Much is stiff and stilted, and of interest mainly for its efficient, succinct expression of ideas—political, philosophical, satirical. But at times his feelings carry him to a more poignant expression, which dominates and gives life to an entire poem. The disaster of the Lisbon earthquake in 1755 led him to write one of his most passionate protests against the senseless tragedies which afflict mankind. In the opening lines of his poem he reproaches the 'philosophers' for their detached, theoretical comments on the disaster and its cruel effects:

'Poem on the Lisbon Disaster' (1756)
An enquiry into the maxim, 'whatever is, is right'.

> Oh wretched man, earth-fated to be cursed;
> Abyss of plagues, and miseries the worst!
> Horrors on horrors, griefs on griefs must show,
> That man's the victim of unceasing woe,
> And lamentations which inspire my strain,
> Prove the philosophers' belief is vain.
> Approach in crowds, and meditate awhile
> Yon shattered walls, and view each ruined pile,
> Women and children heaped up mountain high,
> Limbs crushed which under ponderous marble lie;
> Wretches unnumbered in the pangs of death,
> Who mangled, torn, and panting for their breath,
> Buried beneath their sinking roofs expire,
> And end their wretched lives in torments dire.
> Say, when you hear their piteous, half-formed cries,
> Or from their ashes see the smoke arise,
> Say, will you then eternal laws maintain,
> Which God to cruelties like these constrain?
> Whilst you these facts replete with horror view,
> Will you maintain death to their crimes was due?

23

And can you then impute a sinful deed
To babes who on their mothers' bosoms bleed?
Was then more vice in fallen Lisbon found,
Than Paris, where voluptuous joys abound?
Was less debauchery to London known,
Where opulence luxurious holds her throne?
Earth Lisbon swallows; the light sons of France
Protract the feast, or lead the sprightly dance.

(Cf. 22, 43)

10 The ode: the death of a friend

The public disaster at Lisbon shook Voltaire to the depth of his being. He knew private grief as well. The sister of Frederick of Prussia, Wilhelmina, Margravine of Bayreuth, was a friend of Voltaire's, and showed her friendship at an important time. When Voltaire withdrew—or rather escaped—from Frederick's court at Potsdam, she did her utmost to reconcile the two men, frequently urged Voltaire to stay at her court at Bayreuth, and was eventually able to establish at least a truce between Frederick and Voltaire. The sorrow of both men at her death helped to re-establish some measure of their earlier friendship, and Frederick asked Voltaire to compose an ode in her memory. She died in 1758, at a time when the violence of the Seven Years' War was at its peak. These are the final stanzas of the 'Ode on the Death of Her Royal Highness Madame the Margravine of Bayreuth' (1759):

O noble slaughterers, o victims for a fee,
Who fear disgrace and overcome your fear,
And urge each other on towards a bloody foe,
O you who'd flee, did you but dare,
And die at last for honour's name:
One woman, one Princess,
Tranquil and wise,

Who scorned blind fate's haphazard blows,
Endured life's ills without complaint,
And fearlessly accepted death's cold stare,
This single soul was braver than you all.

But who will sing your loyalty to friends,
That finest virtue, great heart's pride,
That sacred flame which fired your noble soul,
Purer and more pure at misfortune's hand.
Shame on those common souls,
Whose feelings, unlike yours, contract or swell
As wax or wane their comforts and their cash,
Those weathercocks, that swerve and turn
With every changing breeze.

O endless tears unquenchable are due,
A hand, a brush more noble and more skilled
Shall paint your dear, august nobility,
Your virtues, and your worth.
Our children's children shall remember you.
I in my shaky days, decrepit and unsure,
My trembling hand in grief is raised
To write these letters on your grave:
HERE LIES A FRIEND INDEED.

11   *History: the picture of an age*

This extract from Voltaire's *Remarks on History* (1742)
shows his view that change and improvement are possible.
The qualities of liberty, tolerance and intellectual enquiry
which he praised in England can be seen at work, but the
many other forces which shape—or mis-shape—the modern
world are also clearly perceived.

It is my view, if one is to take advantage of the present
age, one's life should on no account be spent in blind in-
fatuation with the ancient fables. I would advise a young

man to have a smattering of these remote times; but I should wish the serious study of history to begin in the time when it becomes truly interesting for ourselves: it seems to me that this is near the end of the fifteenth century. Printing, invented at that very time, begins to make such study less uncertain. The face of Europe changes; the Turks, spreading across its surface, expel the arts from Constantinople; these are led to flourish in Italy, are established in France, and come to polish England, Germany and the north. A new religion separates half Europe from its obedience to the Pope. A new system of politics is established. With the aid of the compass, Africa is circumnavigated; and trade with China becomes easier than it is between Paris and Madrid. America is discovered; a new world is conquered, and our own is almost entirely changed; Christian Europe becomes a kind of vast republic, in which the balance of power is better established than it was in Greece. All its parts are linked by an unceasing correspondence, despite the wars which rise through royal ambition, and even despite wars of religion, more destructive still. The arts, which form the glory of all states, are raised to a level never known in Greece or Rome. Here then is the history which all must know. In this one finds no chimerical predictions, nor lying oracles, nor false miracles, nor senseless fables; all here is true, even the little details, which are a concern only to little minds. It is all related to us, all that has happened is for us to observe. The silver plate on which we take our meals, our furniture, our needs, our latest pleasures, every day each thing reminds us that America and the East Indies—and in consequence, all parts of the entire world—have been brought together, for some two and a half centuries, by the labours of our fathers. Each step we take brings home to us the change which has taken place in the world since then. Here, one finds a hundred towns, once subject to the Pope, and which have become free. There, the privileges of the whole of Germany have been set for a period. Here, the finest of all republics grows in a land which the sea threatens to

overwhelm each day. England has united true freedom
with royalty; Sweden imitates her (though Denmark does
not imitate Sweden). Whether I travel in Germany, in
France, or in Spain, everywhere I find the marks of the
long-drawn strife between the houses of Austria and Bour-
bon, united by so many treaties, of which every one has
led to fatal wars. No individual in the whole of Europe
has remained untouched in some way by all these changes.
And after this, should we busy ourselves with Salmanasar
and with Mardokempad, or study the dates of the Persian
Cayamarrat, and of Sabaco Methophis? A grown man,
dealing with serious things, does not go back to the tales
his nurse told him, when he was a child.

12   Intellectual progress: the great achievement

In the *Age of Louis XIV* there are many sombre passages
to do with war, devastation and failure, but Voltaire sets
these against a picture of triumphant artistic, cultural and
scientific achievement. This intellectual advance was to be
the firm base for the 'enlightened' attitudes of Voltaire's
own age.

We have hinted often enough in the course of this
history, that the public disasters of which it is composed,
and which follow one another almost without interruption,
are at length erased from the registers of time. The details
and the motives of politics recede and are forgotten. The
fine laws, institutions and monuments produced by the
sciences and by the arts remain for ever.
    The crowd of foreigners who travel today to Rome, not
as pilgrims, but as men of taste, care little about Gregory
VII or Boniface VIII; they admire the temples which
Bramante and Michaelangelo have erected, the paintings by
Raphael, the sculptures by the Berninis; if they are of a
lively mind, they read Ariosto and Tasso, and they respect
the ashes of Galileo. In England, they speak briefly of

Cromwell, while no one any longer discusses the wars of the Roses; but the work of Newton is material for years of study; it is no surprise to read in his epitaph that 'he was the glory of the human race', and in this country it would be surprising indeed were one to see the ashes of any statesman honoured with such praise.

I wish that I could do justice here to all the great men who, like Newton, have made their country illustrious in the last century. I have called this century the age of Louis XIV, not merely because this monarch gave more protection to the arts than did all the kings together who were his contemporaries, but also because he saw the entire generations of the princes of Europe three times renewed. I have set the limits of this epoch at a few years before Louis XIV, and a few years after him; it is in effect in this space of time that the human mind has made its greatest progress.

Age of Louis XIV, Ch. xxxiv—passage added in 1756.

Cf. 7.

13   *An aspect of the Inquisition*

Beside the triumphs, there were the abominations. The following passage describes in detail a part of the ceremony of an *auto-da-fé*, which is to reappear in *Candide* (cf. 22). Characteristically, Voltaire uses the isolated incident to introduce general observations—and once again, tolerance is his theme.

But these melancholy effects of the Inquisition are a trifle in comparison to those public sacrifices called *Auto da Fé*, or acts of faith, and to the shocking barbarities that precede them.

A priest in a white surplice, or a monk who has vowed meekness and humility, causes his fellow creatures to be put to the torture in a dismal dungeon. A stage is erected in the public marketplace, where the condemned prisoners are conducted to the stake, attended with a train of monks and religious confraternities. They sing psalms, say mass, and butcher mankind. Were a native of Asia to come to Madrid upon the day of an execution of this sort, it would be impossible for him to tell whether it was a rejoicing, a religious feast, a sacrifice, or a massacre; and yet it is all this together. The kings, whose presence alone in other cases is the harbinger of mercy, assist at this spectacle uncovered, lower seated than the inquisitors, and behold their subject expiring in the flames. The Spaniards reproached Montezuma with immolating his captives to his gods; what would he have said had he beheld an *Auto da Fé*?

Essay on Universal History, Ch. cxl (1756).

14   A Prussian victory

The battle of Rossbach in 1757 was decisive in establishing Frederick's superior position in Europe. Voltaire tells the 'story' of the battle, but weaves into this account many other elements, which reveal the intricacies and interrelationships of events, and the breadth of Voltaire's historical vision. At the beginning, Frederick's military and political position was almost hopeless, and he thought seriously of committing suicide.

He was liable to be surrounded on one side by the army of marshal Richelieu, and, on the other side, by that of the Empire, while the Austrians and Russians entered Silesia; indeed, his ruin seemed so certain, that the Aulic council, without hesitation, declared that he had incurred the ban of the Empire, and that he was deprived of all his fiefs, rights, favours, privileges, &c. It was then that he appeared to despair of his fortune, and only looked for a glorious death; but such was his equanimity and courage, that, while he was in the greatest perplexity, he wrote a kind of philosophical testament in French verse. This is a singular anecdote.

When Frederick was surrounded by so many enemies, he took the resolution to die sword-in-hand in the ranks of the army of the prince de Soubise; but, at the same time, took every measure to conquer him.

After reconnoitring the army of France, and the Circles [German and Austrian allies of the French], he immediately retreated before them in order to possess himself of an advantageous situation. Prince Hilbourghausen was resolved to attack him, and his opinion of course prevailed, because the French were only auxiliaries. They therefore marched between Rossbach and Metzbourg to attack the Prussian army, which was apparently encamped; but, all of a sudden, the tents were struck, and the Prussians appeared in order of battle, between two eminences lined with artillery.

This unexpected sight intimidated the French and Imperialists. For several years it had been proposed to exercise the French troops after the Prussian method; afterwards several evolutions had been altered in the exercise, so that the French soldier did not know what he was doing; his old way of fighting was changed, and he was not perfect in the new. When he saw the Prussians advance in that singular order, unknown almost every where else, he imagined he saw his masters. The king of Prussia's artillery was also better served, and much better posted than that of his enemies. The troops of the Circles fled almost without engaging; the French cavalry were dispersed in an instant by the Prussian cannon; a panic fear spread every where, and the French infantry retired in disorder before six battalions of Prussians. In fact, this was not a battle, but a whole army which offered to fight, and then dispersed. History has hardly any examples of a similar action; only two regiments of Swiss remained in the field, and the prince de Soubise went through the middle of the firing, to make them retreat with deliberation.... This strange battle entirely changed the face of affairs....

Age of Louis XV, Ch. xxxiii (1768).

Hatreds

'Who was that great pig, said Candide, who spoke so ill to
me of the piece by which I was so much affected, and of
the players who gave me so much pleasure?—A living
scourge, answered the Abbé, one who gets his livelihood
by abusing every new book and play; he abominates to
see any one meet with success, like eunuchs, who detest
every one that has, what they lack; he is one of those
vipers in literature who nourish themselves on slime and
venom; a pamphlet-monger ... —A pamphlet-monger!
said Candide, what is that?—Why, a pamphlet-monger,
replied the Abbé, is a writer of pamphlets, a *Fréron*.'

Candide, Ch. xxii.

'Esprit' : wit, intelligence, a resourceful, inventive, humorous, lively mind. Those are the positive aspects of 'esprit',
and Voltaire possessed them all. But Voltaire's *esprit*—
and was there ever a Frenchman more gifted with *esprit*
than Voltaire?—had negative qualities too—mockery,
malice and spite.

One rarely succeeds without arousing envy, and in this
Voltaire's success was no exception. One rarely attacks
an institution—the Church, say, or the Government—with-

out wounding some of the institution's members. Voltaire's attacks were nothing if not effective. They wounded, and deeply. And so, soon in his career, and for the rest of his life, Voltaire made himself enemies, who attacked him often and in many ways. In 1726 the Chevalier de Rohan set his lackeys to thrash Voltaire in the street, in 1753 Frederick of Prussia had Voltaire ignominiously detained for weeks in Frankfurt; many times the French government had Voltaire exiled, from the Court, from Paris, out of France altogether; many times, and in many places, his works were publicly burnt, as a sign of the total disapproval in which the authorities held them and their author. And the spokesmen of the Government and of the Church—politicians, journalists, priests—attacked him in their writings.

Voltaire could not exile his enemies, or have them thrashed or imprisoned. But he could write about them, and he did so with an *esprit* whose unforgiving sharpness is one of his most striking qualities. Though the world may have forgotten Elie Fréron, literary critic and journalist, it remembers what Voltaire said about him in *Candide*.

15 Maupertuis

P.-L. Moreau de Maupertuis (1698-1759), scientist and mathematician, was made President of the Berlin Academy by Frederick of Prussia. Voltaire was at first reasonably friendly with him, but then quarrelled, and while staying at Potsdam wrote a pamphlet, the *History of Dr Akakia* (1752), in which he cruelly attacked the whole range of Maupertuis' scientific interests and ambitions. Seven years later, Voltaire recalls some of the subjects which Maupertuis had discussed:

... but I wished [before leaving Potsdam] to enjoy the

pleasure of laughing at a book Maupertuis had just printed.
It was the best of opportunities, for never had any thing
appeared so ridiculous or absurd. The good man seriously
proposed to travel directly to the two Poles to dissect the
heads of giants, and discover the nature of the soul by the
texture of the brain; to build a city, and make the inhabitants all speak Latin; to sink a pit to the centre of the
earth; to cure the sick, by plastering them over with gum-
resin; and, finally, to prophesy, by enthusiastically inflating
the fancy.

The king laughed, I laughed, every body laughed at his
book ...

Memoirs of M. de Voltaire (1759).

16 *Frederick*

Maupertuis' protector Frederick felt obliged to intervene,
and had Voltaire's pamphlet publicly burnt by the hang-
man in Berlin. Relations between Voltaire and the king
were already strained—when another courtier had spoken
enviously to Frederick of Voltaire's favoured position,
Frederick had replied, 'Don't be concerned; one squeezes
an orange, and then, when you have drunk the juice, you
throw away the peel.' In turn, Voltaire said biting things
about Frederick. Frederick wrote indifferent poetry in
French, and one of Voltaire's chief occupations at Potsdam was the correction and improvement of these verses.
In exasperation, Voltaire remarked, 'Will he never stop
sending me his dirty linen to wash?' Naturally, this soon
reached Frederick's ears. Frederick took his revenge cruelly
enough, making it immensely difficult for Voltaire to leave
Potsdam in 1753, and then humiliating him at Frankfurt.
But Voltaire was not the only victim of this royal malice.
The intellectuals at Frederick's court all suffered in various
ways. In his *Memoirs* Voltaire mocks both the king and his
victims:

33

It is well known how much must be borne from kings, but Frederick was too free in the abuse of his prerogative. All society has its laws, except the society of the Lion and the Lamb. Frederick continually failed in the first of these laws; which is, to say nothing disobliging of any of the company. He often used to ask his chamberlain, Pöllnitz, if he would not willingly change his religion a fourth time, and offer to pay a hundred crowns down for his conversion. 'Good God, my dear Pöllnitz, he would say, I have forgot the name of that person at the Hague, whom you cheated by selling him base for pure silver; let me beg of you to assist my memory a little.' He treated poor d'Argens much in the same way, and yet these two victims remained. Pöllnitz having wasted his fortune, was obliged to swallow serpents for bread, and had no other food; and d'Argens had no property in the world, but his *Jewish Letters*, and his wife, called Cochois, a bad provincial actress, and so ugly she could get no employment at any trade, though she practised several. As for Maupertuis, who had been silly enough to place out his money at Berlin, and not thinking a hundred pistoles better in a free country than a thousand in a despotic one, he had no choice but to wear the fetters which himself had forged.

17   *Jean-Jacques Rousseau*

As with Maupertuis, Voltaire was at first on tolerable terms with Rousseau, but the direction taken by Rousseau's writings in the 1760s—his praise of 'natural' and 'passionate' ways of conduct and education, which diverged from the rational and society-centred attitudes of most *philosophes*—seemed to Voltaire a turning away from the true rational approach of an enlightened man, and indeed an attitude bordering on madness. Rousseau's disapproval of the theatre, his novel the *New Héloïse* (1761) and his treatise on education, *Emile* (1761), provoked Voltaire's scorn.

Let us forgive Jean-Jacques when he writes but to contradict himself; when, after his having given a comedy, hissed off the stage at Paris, he censures those who have plays acted a hundred leagues from that town; when he lays out for patrons and abuses them; when he declaims against romances and writes romances, of which the hero is a silly preceptor, who receives charity from a Swiss girl whom he has got with child, and who goes to spend her money at a bawdy-house in Paris; let us leave him to his thinking that he has surpassed Fénelon and Xenophon in his plan of educating a young man of quality in the trade of a joiner: these insipid absurdities do not deserve a warrant to take him into custody; the cells of Bedlam are sufficient, with some good broths, blood-letting, and a proper regimen.

The Man of Forty Crowns (1768).

18 *Berthier: enemy of the* philosophes

G.-F. Berthier (1704-82) was a Jesuit, and one of the editors of the Jesuit periodical, the *Journal de Trévoux*, which had attacked Voltaire for his hostility towards the Catholic church, and was also bitterly opposed to the great *Encyclopédie* which the *philosophes*—Diderot, d'Alembert, Voltaire and many others—were publishing. In 1759 the Jesuits were instrumental in having the publication of the *Encyclopédie* suspended, and Voltaire wrote a series of scathing attacks against Berthier as a result. In the *Account of the Illness, Confession, Death and Apparition of the Jesuit Berthier* (1759) Voltaire presented the luckless Berthier with the story of his own death. Here is the opening stage of his illness. Berthier is supposed to be travelling to Versailles in a coach with friar Coutu. In their luggage are various copies of the *Journal de Trévoux*.

On the way Berthier felt a trifle queasy; his head felt

heavy, and he yawned again and again. 'It's very odd, he said to Coutu, I've never yawned so much.'

[Coutu began to yawn too.] The coachman looked round, and, seeing them yawning like this, began to yawn as well; the disease affected all the passers-by, and the people yawned in all the neighbouring houses. What an effect the mere presence of a learned man can sometimes produce!

Meanwhile Berthier was seized by a cold sweat. 'It's very odd, he said, I feel ice-cold.—I know what you mean,' said his companion the friar. 'What? You know what I mean!' said Berthier. 'What d'you mean by that?—Well, I'm frozen too,' said Coutu. 'I'm going to sleep,' said Berthier. 'I'm not surprised,' said the other. 'Why d'you say that?' asked Berthier. 'Well, I'm falling asleep too,' said his companion.

[Sleeping, they reach Versailles, and Coutu is roused, but Berthier gets colder than ever.] Several doctors from the Court, who were returning from dinner, passed near the coach, and they were asked to have a look at the sick man. One of them, after feeling his pulse, went off saying that he didn't get involved in medicine any more, not since he had come to Court. Another, after looking at him more thoroughly, stated that the malady stemmed from the gall-bladder, which was continually over-worked; a third maintained that it was all because of the brain, which was too empty.

While they were discussing the case, the patient got worse, his convulsions began to show ominous signs, and the three fingers used to hold a pen were already completely clenched. Then a senior doctor, who had studied under Mead and Boerhaave [doctors admired by Voltaire], and who had a deeper understanding than the others, opened Berthier's mouth with a feeding-spoon, and, after a careful consideration of the odour which came out, pronounced him to have been poisoned.

At this, everyone cried out in alarm. 'Yes, gentlemen, he went on, he has been poisoned; you need only feel his skin, to see that the exhalations of a chill poison have penetrated through the pores; and I would hold this to be a worse poison than a mixture of hemlock, black hellebore, opium, solanum and jusquiam. Coachman, you didn't by any chance put a parcel in your coach for our apothecaries?— Oh no, sir,' replied the coachman. 'This here is the only package which I put in the coach—and by the Rev. Father's orders.' Then he rummaged in his trunk, and brought out a couple of dozen copies of the *Journal de Trévoux*. 'Well, gentlemen, was I wrong?'

All who were there admired his prodigious wisdom; everyone realized the origin of the malady. At once, in front of the patient, they burnt the pernicious parcel, and since the heavy particles were lightened by the action of the fire, Berthier was somewhat relieved; but, as the illness had made great progress, and his head was infected, the danger was still present. The doctor had the idea of making him swallow a page of the *Encyclopédie*, taken in white wine, in order to free the humours of his clotted bile: and this produced a copious evacuation. But his head still remained dreadfully heavy, his vertigo continued, and the few words he was able to articulate had no sense in them; for two hours he remained in this state, after which they were obliged to have recourse to confession.

Humorous, malicious, easy to read, almost a 'story'— and also an attack. We smile at the *esprit*—and we realize that the satire has succeeded.

Candide

'The best of all possible worlds.' *Candide*, Ch. ii.

Gustave Flaubert called *Candide* a résumé of all that Voltaire wrote. Certainly this short work brings together practically all his preoccupations, passions, sympathies and hatreds, and I think it holds so central a place in his writings that each group of extracts in this book is headed by a quotation from *Candide*. The wonder of *Candide* is that although it has so many and such varied allusions to Voltaire's interests—the horror of the world (war, famine, plague, earthquakes, pirates, slavery, cannibals, traitors, thieves, murderers, perverts, oppressors and fanatics of every kind)—individuals (Fréron, Frederick the Great, Admiral Byng, Maupertuis)—and a host of separate subjects (the Church, scientific enquiries, the arts, the Parisian scene, philosophy, history, foreign travel)—in spite of this diversity the work is a triumphant whole, directed uniquely at *exposing* folly, hypocrisy and horror, and through mockery and laughter at destroying our complacency. But *Candide* is also a short work, and concentrates ferociously on the negative aspects of life. In this respect it is not

representative of the whole of Voltaire—his many positive
sides, and in particular his constructive social sympathies,
are represented only in the last, resounding 'but we must
cultivate our garden'. Voltaire was to follow the advice for
the rest of his life—'Champion of the oppressed' shows
some of the ways in which he set about the task.

Passages 19 and 28 are not from *Candide*, but serve as
introduction and conclusion.

19   *The attack on Optimism*

The tragic earthquake which destroyed a great part of
Lisbon in 1755 convinced Voltaire that the world was not
—as cheerful 'Optimists' maintained—essentially a happy
place. We must not deceive ourselves. Candide, the young
hero of the novel, will be taken round most of the world
to learn this very lesson.

... convinced of man's unhappiness, he [the author] protests against the abuse which may be made of that old
axiom 'All is right'. He accepts that sad and yet more
ancient truth, known to all men, that 'there is evil in the
world'; he admits that the phrase 'All is right' taken in an
absolute sense and without hope in the future is no more
than an insult to the sorrows of our lives.

Preface to 'Poem on the Lisbon Earthquake' (1756).
Cf. 43.

20   *What Candide believes*

Candide, the most innocent of pupils, learns the philosophy
of Optimism from Pangloss—germanic, verbose, deaf to
everything except the sound of his own voice. To Pangloss
everything, however awful it may seem to us, is really
excellent. Correction—*perfect*!

Pangloss was professor of metaphysico-theologo-cosmolo-

39

nigology. He could prove most admirably, that there is no effect without a cause, and that in this world, the best of all possible worlds, the baron's castle was the most magnificent of castles, and his lady the best of baronesses that could possibly exist.

'It is demonstrable, said he, that things cannot be otherwise than they are: for all things having been created for some end, they must consequently be created for the best. Observe, that the nose is formed for spectacles, and therefore we come to wear spectacles. The legs are visibly designed for stockings, and therefore we come to wear stockings. Stones were made to be hewn, and to construct castles; therefore my lord has a magnificent castle: for the greatest baron in the province ought to be the best lodged. Swine were intended to be eat; therefore we eat pork all the year round; and they who assert, that every thing is right, do not express themselves correctly; they should say that every thing is for the best.'

Candide, Ch. i. Cf. 43.

21   *The heroic glory of war*

Candide, driven out into the world, is caught by a press-gang, becomes a soldier (or 'hero') in the army of the Bulgares (the Prussians, ruled by Frederick the Great), and takes part in man's most dreadful activity. Is it all for the best?

There was never any thing so gallant, so well accoutered, so brilliant, and so well disposed, as the two armies were. Trumpets, fifes, haut-boys, drums, and cannon, made such music, as the devil himself never heard in hell. The cannonading first of all laid flat about six thousand men on each side; the musket-balls swept away out of the best of worlds, nine or ten thousand ruffians that infected the surface of the earth. The bayonet was next a sufficient reason for the death of several thousands. The whole might amount to thirty thousand souls. Candide trembled like a philosopher, and concealed himself as well as he could during this heroic butchery.

At length, while the two kings were causing Te Deum to be sung in each of their camps, Candide took a resolution to go and reason somewhere else about effects and causes. After he had passed over heaps of dead or dying men, the first place he came to was a neighbouring village, which belonged to the Abares, and had been set on fire by the Bulgares, according to the laws of war. Here you might see old men covered with wounds, who beheld their wives, hugging their children to their bloody breasts, massacred before their faces. There you might behold young virgins with their bellies ripped open, and breathing of their last, after they had satisfied the natural wants of Bulgarian heroes; while others, half burnt in the flames, begged to be dispatched out of the world. The earth was strewed with the brains, arms, and legs of dead men.

Candide made all the haste he could to another village, which belonged to the Bulgares; and there he found that the heroic Abares had acted the same tragedy. From thence continuing to walk over shattered palpitating limbs, or through ruined buildings, he arrived at last beyond the seat of war, with a few provisions in his knapsack, and miss Cunégonde always in his heart.

Candide, Ch. iii.

22   *The Inquisition punishes the enemies of the Church*

After the Lisbon earthquake, a solemn 'auto-da-fé' or act of faith is held, to 'preserve the kingdom from utter ruin'. Suitable victims are rounded up and imprisoned—Candide and Pangloss included—and duly punished, in public ceremony. The 'Biscayner' was thought to have married his godmother, and the 'two men who refused to eat hog's lard' were ex-Jews. With these punishments, how can this world be the best?

They were conducted to separate apartments, extremely fresh and cool, being never incommoded by the sun: eight days after they were dressed in a *sanbenito*, and their heads were crowned with paper mitres. The mitre and sanbenito belonging to Candide were painted with inverse flames, and with devils that had neither tails nor claws: but Pangloss's devils had claws, and the flames were upright. In this habit they marched in procession, and heard a very pathetic sermon, which was followed by an anthem set to music. Candide was whipt in cadence, while they were singing; the Biscayner, and the two men who refused to eat hog's lard, were burnt; and Pangloss, though contrary to custom, was hanged. The same day the earth again sustained a most violent concussion.

Candide, terrified and amazed at the shocking bloody scene, said to himself with some trepidation: 'If this is the best of possible worlds, what must we think of the rest?'

Candide, Ch. vi. Cf. 9, 13.

23 *The spoils of war: a quarrel*

The senseless destruction of war is paralleled by the killings which are part of piracy. Female captives, like the princess of Palestrina who tells the story, are the cause of endless carnage. Note Voltaire's dig at the religious propriety observed throughout the massacres.

'At length I saw all our Italian women and my mother mangled and torn in pieces by the monsters who contended for them. The captives, my companions, the Moors who took us, the soldiers, the sailors, the blacks, the whites, the mulattoes, and lastly, my captain himself, were all slain, and I remained alone expiring upon a heap of dead bodies. The like barbarous scenes were transacted every day all over the country, through an extent of three hundred leagues, and yet they never missed the five prayers a-day, ordained by Mahomet.'

Candide, Ch. xi.

24   In Eldorado: the ideal religion

In South America Candide and his servant Cacambo reach
the secret land of Eldorado. Here a perfect society exists,
safe from the destruction of ordinary mortals. Naturally,
their religion is perfect too, and the Old Man, or Sage, cannot understand the point of Candide's questions. But Voltaire's contemporaries could—they knew that, indirectly,
he was attacking abuses in the Church of Rome.

Cacambo humbly asked, what was the established religion
in Eldorado? The old man, reddening once more, made
answer: 'Can there be two religions? We have the religion
of the whole world; we worship God from morning till
night.—Do you worship but one God?' said Cacambo, who
still acted as interpreter in representing Candide's doubts.
'Sure, says the old man, there are not two, nor three, nor
four. I must confess, the people from your side of the
world ask very extraordinary questions.' Candide was not
yet tired of interrogating the good old man; he wanted to
know in what manner they prayed to God in Eldorado.
'We do not pray to him at all, said the respectable sage; we
have nothing to ask of him; he has given us all we need,
and we incessantly return him thanks.' Candide having a
curiosity to see the priests, asked where they were? At
which the good old man smiling, said: 'My friends, we are
all priests; the king and all the heads of families sing solemn
canticles of thanksgiving every morning, accompanied by
five or six thousand musicians.—What! have you no monks
to teach, to dispute, to govern, to cabal, and to burn
people that are not of their opinion?—We must be mad,
indeed, if that were the case, said the old man; here we are
all of one opinion, and we know not what you mean by
monks.'

Candide, Ch. xviii. Cf. 34, 39.

25   *The price of sugar*

Owners of slaves in the plantations of South America and
the Indies could inflict fearsome punishments for trivial
offences; slaves had little to live for. The sight of this slave,
mutilated and in despair, finally broke Candide's faith in
'Optimism', which he now derides.

As they drew near the town, they saw a negroe stretched
upon the ground, with only one moiety of his habit, that
is, of his blue linen drawers; the poor man had lost his left
leg and his right arm. 'Good God! said Candide, in Dutch,
what art thou doing there, friend, in that shocking con-
dition?—I am waiting for my master mynheer Vanderdendur, the famous merchant, answered the negroe.—Was
it mynheer Vanderdendur, said Candide, that used thee in
this manner?—Yes, sir, said the negroe, it is the custom of
the country. They give us a pair of linen drawers for our
whole garment twice a year. When we work at the sugar-
canes, and the mill snatches hold of a finger, they cut off
our hand: and when we attempt to run away, they cut
off our leg: both cases have happened to me. This is the
price of the sugar you eat in Europe. . . .'
   'O Pangloss! cried Candide, you never thought of this
horrid scene; I can share your belief no more, I must re-
nounce your optimism at last.—What is optimism? said
Cacambo.—Alas! said Candide, it is the folly of maintain-
ing that every thing is right, when it is wrong!'

Candide, Ch. xix. Cf. 43.

26   *What is Candide to do?*

Candide and his friends have reached a small farm in the
neighbourhood of Constantinople. Outside, the world goes
on as usual—ambitious, violent, unreliable—but among
themselves, Candide and his friends have no answer. The
boredom which comes from inactivity is as bad as their

sufferings in the world, here summarized by the Old Woman:

Candide, Martin, and Pangloss, sometimes disputed about morality and metaphysics. They often saw under the farm windows boats full of effendis, bashaws, and cadis, who were going into banishment to Lemnos, Mitylene, or Erzerum. And they saw other cadis, bashaws, and effendis, coming to supply the place of the exiles, and afterwards exiled in their turn. They saw heads decently impaled, which were to be presented to the Sublime Porte. Such spectacles as these increased the number of their dissertations; and when they did not dispute, time hung so heavy upon their hands, that one day the old woman ventured to say to them: 'I want to know which is worse, to be ravished a hundred times by negro pirates, to have a buttock cut off, to run the gauntlet among the Bulgarians, to be whipped and hanged at an Auto-da-fé, to be dissected, to be a galley-slave; in short, to go through all the miseries that we have undergone, or to stay here and have nothing to do?—It is a very difficult question,' said Candide.

Candide, Ch. xxx.

27   *Candide decides to act*

Pangloss talks too much. But everyone can 'do his bit', each according to his ability. *Work* is the solution—constructive, sensible, properly distributed, directed towards a modest and practical goal:

'I know also, said Candide, that we must cultivate our garden.—You are in the right, said Pangloss; for when our first parent was placed in the garden of Eden, he was put there *ut operaretur eum*, to cultivate it; which shews that man was not born to be idle.—Let us work, said Martin, without disputing, it is the only way to render life tolerable.'

45

Hereupon the whole society entered into this laudable decision, according to their different abilities. Their little piece of ground produced them a plentiful crop. Cunégonde indeed was very ugly, but she became an excellent pastry-cook, while Paquette worked at embroidery, and the old woman looked after the linen. They were all, not excepting friar Giroflée, of some service or other; for he made a good carpenter and became a very honest man. Pangloss used sometimes to say to Candide 'There is a concatenation of events in this best of all possible worlds; for if you had not been kicked out of a magnificent castle, on account of miss Cunégonde; ... you would not be here to eat preserved citrons and pistachio nuts.—All that is very well, answered Candide, but we must cultivate our garden.'

Candide, Ch. xxx. Cf. 44.

28 *The search for personal security*

The fiction of Candide is backed at every point by real events—historical or personal. Voltaire, long the victim of persecution, and despairing of the world and the tyrannies of kings, acquired several 'bolt-holes' in and near to Switzerland where he could live comfortably and write freely. Soon after buying the properties described below, he purchased a large estate at Ferney, just inside the French border but still within easy reach of Geneva. This was the immediate 'garden' which he was to 'cultivate' for the rest of his life.

I bought ... a small estate of about sixty acres, which was sold me at double the price it would have cost near Paris; but pleasure can never be bought too dearly; the house is pretty, and convenient; the prospect from it is charming; it surprises and never tires you. On one side, you see the lake of Geneva, and on the other, the town.... I have an even lovelier house and a more extensive view at Lausanne; but my house near Geneva is much more pleasant. In these two dwellings, I have that which kings do not grant—or

46

rather, that which they take away, repose and liberty ...

All the commodities that one could require of life in the way of furnishings, carriages, and food and drink are available in my two houses; the company of pleasant, intelligent people fills such moments as are left over from my work and the care of my health. ...

While in my retreat I enjoyed the most pleasant life one could imagine. I had the modest and philosophic satisfaction of seeing that the kings of Europe did not partake of this happy tranquillity, and of concluding that the situation of a private individual is often to be preferred to that of the greatest monarchs.

Memoirs of M. de Voltaire (1759). Cf. 16.

L'Infâme

'What! have you no monks to teach, to dispute, to govern, to cabal, and to burn people that are not of their opinion?' *Candide*, Ch. xviii.

'Écrasons l'infâme'—'Crush the infamous thing': this phrase of Voltaire's, as famous as the last line of *Candide*, comes into his writings in 1759. It was first suggested in a letter of 18 May 1759, from Frederick to Voltaire, and Voltaire quickly adopted it as his own, sometimes even using it as his signature instead of his own name. 'L'infâme' really refers to the evil of fanaticism, of corruption and intolerance within the Church, rather than to the Christian religion as a whole. Indeed, Voltaire quite often pointed out the positive social value and usefulness of the minor clergy, especially the parish priests. But his attack on abuses within the Church stemming from fanaticism and intolerance was relentless, and his indignation led him at times to condemn Christianity outright, as in his letter to Frederick of 5 January 1767, when he declared, 'As long as there are rogues and fools, there will be religions. Our own is, without gainsay, the most ridiculous, absurd and bloody which has ever infected the world.'

Although the phrase 'écrasons l'infâme' dates only from 1759, the time of *Candide*, his hostility to these evils goes back to his earliest writings, and appears many times in the selections in this volume (e.g. 13, 18, 22, 47). The two main extracts quoted below refer to monks, whom Voltaire considered particularly non-productive, indeed a negative body. But 'l'infâme' in his writings has many other aspects as well—the Inquisition, the Crusades, unjust or illogical ecclesiastical privileges, fanatical sects within the Church (Jesuits and Jansenists attracted most scorn), and ignorant, unjust, prejudiced or fanatical actions by the Church—which could fill several sturdy volumes.

29 *Shakespeare—eighteenth-century style*

In his *Letters Concerning the English Nation*, Voltaire included several pages on Shakespeare, incorporating a translation of Hamlet's soliloquy 'To be, or not to be'. Voltaire's French version is faithful, except for one insertion: in the passage 'For who would bear the whips and scorns of time, /.../ But that the dread of something after death ...' he adds to the list of life's indignities the obligation 'de nos prêtres menteurs bénir l'hypocrisie', 'to bless our lying priests' hypocrisy'. The addition is characteristic of his inclination to 'slip in' anti-clerical comments, even in the most unexpected places.

30 *Monks*

In *Candide*, brother Giroflée remarks bitterly that 'jealousy, discord, and fury reside in our convent' (Ch. xxiv), emphasizing the unwillingness of so many monks and nuns to enter their profession at that time. Elsewhere Voltaire writes about the cost to the nation of these communities, whose wealth often contrasted savagely with the poverty

49

of the peasants, or even with the fixed, and inadequate stipend of the parish priests.

A few years ago, when we were passing through Burgundy in the company of monsieur Evrard, whom you all know, we saw a vast palace being built, of which one part was well under way. I asked, to which prince it belonged. A mason replied that it belonged to monseigneur the abbot of Cîteaux, and that the agreement had been for seventeen thousand *livres*, but that it would probably cost much more.

I blessed God, that he should have thus enabled his servants to erect so fine a monument, and to disburse so much money in the region. 'Are you serious?' asked monsieur Evrard, 'Isn't it shameful that idleness should be rewarded by rents of two hundred and fifty thousand livres, while the devotion of a poor country curate is punished by a "just stipend" of a hundred crowns? Don't you find this discrepancy the most unjust, the most odious thing you've ever seen? What does the state receive, when a monk lives in a palace worth two million? Twenty poor officers' families, sharing those two million, could each have a decent estate, and could provide new officers for the king. The little monks, who are today just useless subjects of one of their own monks, whom they have elected, would become members of the state, instead of being, as they are, no more than gnawing parasites.'

I answered monsieur Evrard. 'You're going too far, and too fast. What you say will doubtless be achieved in two or three hundred years. Be patient.—That's the very reason why I can't just be patient, he replied, because it will take at least two or three centuries; I'm tired of all the abuses I can see: I feel as if I were walking in the Libyan desert, where, if the lions aren't devouring you, it's the insects that suck your blood.'

Pot-Pourri (1765).

31 Monks again

The hero of Voltaire's story *The Man of Forty Crowns* (1768) has a very small fixed income. Like Candide, he is a naïve man, and the contrast between his own meagre resources and the wealth of that nearby abbey perplexes him.

He asked me why the monks were so rich, while he was poor. 'Are they more useful to their country than I am?— No, dear neighbour.—Do they, like me, contribute at least to the population of it?—No, at least not to appearance.— Do they cultivate the land? Do they defend the state when it is attacked?—No, they pray to God for us.—Well then, I will pray to God for them, and let us share our wealth.

How many of these useful gentry, men and women, may the convents in this kingdom contain?—[...] About ninety thousand. [...]

—You think, then, that it would be doing them a great service to strip them all of their monk's habit?

—They would undoubtedly gain much by it, and the state still more; it would restore to the country a number of subjects, men and women, who have rashly sacrificed their liberty, at an age in which the laws do not allow a capacity of disposing of ten pence a year income. It would be taking these corpses out of their tombs, and afford a true resurrection. Their houses might become hospitals, or be turned into places for manufactures. Population would be increased, all the arts would be better cultivated.... The example of England and so many other states is an evident proof of the necessity of this reformation. What would England do at this time, if, instead of forty thousand seamen, it had forty thousand monks? ... To make a kingdom flourish, there should be the fewest priests and the most artisans possible.

32 Religious wars: fanaticism at its most violent

Later writers in the Romantic period were to see the Cru-

sades as an exotic adventure, the earthly pursuit of a sublime religious ideal, and much of this glamorous conception
remains with us today. But for the eighteenth century, the
Crusades were a proof of man's blind barbarity, the ulti-
mate in intolerance. To exterminate others, in the name of
an unprovable metaphysical truth! Barely less horrible were
the wars of religion which followed the Reformation. Intolerance, fanaticism, murder, again for the sake of the
intangible. Reason, the cherished faculty of the Enlightenment, is ignored. Voltaire's *conte*, *In Praise of Reason* (*Eloge
historique de la raison*, 1774), describes the progress towards
a 'reasonable' society made during the eighteenth century.
But first, a brief comment is needed on the—unreasonable
—horrors of the past:

For many years [during the 'Dark Ages'] we wallowed in
this horrible and base barbarity. The Crusades did nothing
to lift us out. They were madness—of the most universal,
atrocious, ridiculous and unhappy kind. The abominable
madness of civil and holy wars ... followed these remote
Crusades. Reason could not bear to watch. It was a time
when Politics was queen in Rome—she had as ministers
her two sisters, Dishonesty and Greed. Ignorance, Fanaticism and Fury ran throughout Europe to obey her orders;
Poverty followed everywhere they went. Reason hid in a
well, with her daughter Truth. No one knew where this
well was—and had they guessed they would have climbed
down inside it to murder the daughter and her mother.

No wonder the Church saw Voltaire among its fiercest
enemies. Some years after Voltaire's death Collin de Plancy,
writing his *Infernal Dictionary*, listed 'Voltaire' under the
letter 'V', remarking that several authorities 'count him
among the incarnate demons'.

The philosophe

'Why meddle in this? said the dervish; is it any of your business?' *Candide*, Ch. xxx.

Voltaire, more than any other eighteenth-century Frenchman, represents the *philosophe*. We must use the French term, which means, not merely 'philosopher' or student of philosophy, but the man who, through his outlook and behaviour, lives according to rational, calm and humane principles.

33 *A definition*

Voltaire gives us this passage to explain the term:

Philosophe, *a lover of wisdom*, that is to say *of truth*. All *philosophes* have had this double character; throughout antiquity there is not one of them who has not given examples of virtue to man, and lessons of moral truths.... The *philosophe* is never a fanatic, and he does not hold himself up as a prophet, he claims no inspiration from the gods....
    Philosophical Dictionary, article 'Philosophe' (1765).

What are the rational, calm and humane principles which guide a *philosophe*'s behaviour? Just as Voltaire represents the figure of the *philosophe*, so his philosophical attitude is largely representative of the Enlightenment as a whole, and stands in marked contrast to the attitudes of previous centuries. Briefly, Voltaire maintained that, convinced though he was of the existence of God, and of man's need to believe in God, it was impossible for man to discover the answers to metaphysical questions—the nature of the soul, of life after death, of heaven or hell—and therefore any attempt to do so was a waste of time. More serious, any attempt to find out these things, to seek divine revelation, could lead to personal delusion and thence to fanaticism, 'l'infâme'.

Voltaire, then, was a deist—or theist as he sometimes terms it—a man who believes in the existence of God.

34 The deist—or theist: further definition

The definition which follows is worth comparing with the pictures Voltaire draws of the religion of the Quakers, in the *Letters Concerning the English Nation* (1), and of the religion of the inhabitants of Eldorado in *Candide* (24).

The theist is a man firmly convinced of the existence of a supreme Being, who is as good as he is powerful, who has formed all creatures that have extent, that grow, feel and reflect; who perpetuates their species, who punishes their crimes without cruelty, and rewards virtuous actions with kindness.

The theist does not know in what ways God punishes, how he approves, how he pardons; for he is not so rash or forward as to imagine that he can know how God acts; but he knows that God does act, and that he is just ... he believes that Providence extends in all places and through all ages.

United in this principle with the rest of the universe, he belongs to no sect, as they all contradict each other. His religion is the oldest and the most widespread of all; for the simple adoration of a God came before all the systems which the world has devised. He speaks a tongue which all people understand, while they are at odds with each other. He has brothers from Peking to Cayenne, and he numbers all wise men as his brothers. He believes that religion consists neither in the opinions of an incomprehensible metaphysics, nor in vain ceremonies, but in adoration and in justice. To do good—that is his cult; to obey God—that is his doctrine. The Mahometan cries out to him: 'Beware, if you do not make the pilgrimage to Mecca!' 'Woe betide you, a friar says to him, if you do not make a journey to Our Lady of Loretto!' He laughs at Loretto and at Mecca; but he succours the poor, and he defends the oppressed.

Philosophical Dictionary, article 'Theist' (1765).

35   *Metaphysical enquiry: a delusion*

'Why meddle in this?' says the dervish in *Candide*. Again and again Voltaire stresses the impossibility of discovering anything beyond the reach of our rational faculties (cf. 6). Human ability is too limited to unravel the secrets of eternity, which must remain forever hidden. In Voltaire's very first letter to Frederick of Prussia, written on 26 August 1736, the immense, unbridgeable gap between man and the Creator is eloquently described:

... lightning-flashes in the midst of darkest night; this is, I think, all that one may hope from metaphysics. There is nothing to show that the first principles of things have ever been well understood. The mice who dwell in a few wretched holes within a vast edifice know neither, if this edifice is eternal, nor who is its architect, nor why this architect built as he did. They endeavour to stay alive, to populate their holes, and to escape from the destructive animals which pursue them. We are the mice, and the divine architect who has built this universe has not yet, to my knowledge, told his secret to any one of us.

36 Man's weakness and ignorance

Eager though he was to encourage man's rational conduct, Voltaire always insisted on the need to recognize man's relative insignificance in the vastness of the universe. We are but specks upon the surface of the earth, and the earth itself but an atom of mud in the universe as a whole. How can we pretend to omniscience?

I am a feeble creature; at my birth I have neither strength, knowledge nor instinct; I cannot even crawl to my mother's breast, as do other quadrupeds. I only acquire a few ideas, as I acquire a little strength and as my organs begin to unfold themselves. This strength increases in me, till such time as having attained my full growth it daily decreases. This power of conceiving ideas increases in the same manner until its term, and afterwards by degrees insensibly vanishes.

What is that mechanism which increases the strength of my members from hour to hour, as far as the prescribed degree? I am ignorant of it; and those who have passed their whole lives in the research know no more than myself.

What is that other power, which conveys images into my brain, and which preserves them in my memory? Those who are paid to know have only made fruitless enquiries; with regard to first principles we are all in the same state of ignorance as we were in the cradle.

The Ignorant Philosopher, Section ii (1766). Cf. 6.

37 The impertinence of such enquiries

When real work remains to be done—keeping alive, and

'cultivating our garden' in the face of all that the world can offer in the way of disaster and injustice—speculation on the nature of the soul, its relationship to the body and to its Creator is not only impossible (see 34, 35) but it is also an irrelevance, which serious people brush aside.

I have asked some of my own likenesses who cultivate the earth our common mother with great industry, if they felt that they contained two beings? If they had discovered by their philosophy that they possessed within them an immortal substance, and nevertheless formed of nothing, existing without extent, acting upon their nerves without touching them, sent expressly into the belly of their mother six weeks after their conception? They thought that I was jesting, and pursued the cultivation of their land without making me a reply.

The Ignorant Philosopher, Section iii (1766).

38   Man's duty

Man, minute, insignificant, but still a rational being, knows only the immensity, the absolute superiority of his Creator, 'who is as good as he is powerful'. His religious duty then is to worship God, and to do good (cf. 1, 24, 34).

I am already convinced that, not knowing what I am, I cannot know what is my author. I am every instant overwhelmed with my ignorance, and I console myself by incessantly reflecting that it is of no consequence to me to know, whether my master is or is not in the extent of the universe, provided I do nothing against the conscience he has given me. Of all the systems which men have invented to explain the Divinity, which one shall I embrace? None, except that of adoring him.

The Ignorant Philosopher, Section xxiii (1766).

39   *The Chinese: a deist civilization*

The *philosophes* generally believed that Chinese intellectuals, led by Confucius, had achieved a monotheistic religion by rational means, and this example (although it was largely mythical) was held up for comparison with the superstitious and fanatical forms of Christianity to be found in Europe. The Chinese therefore are shown in Voltaire to be deists rather like the inhabitants of Eldorado. In a passage relating to Confucius he writes, 'Never was the adoration of God so pure and holy as in China.... What has been the religion of all reasonable men in China for so many centuries? It is this: "Adore heaven, and be just." '

The Ignorant Philosopher, Section xli (1766).

40 *'Adore heaven, and be just'*

From the beginning, justice was a preoccupation with Voltaire, a principle which seemed essential to the existence of a sane society, and indeed to the construction of the universe. Fanaticism, intolerance, brought with them the denial of justice. In contrast, rational behaviour could only be just, and the *philosophe* prided himself on the pre-eminence of reason and justice in his own conduct.

The notion of what is just appears to me so natural, so universally received by all men, that it is independent of all law, of all compact, of all religion ...

The idea of justice appears to me so much of a truth of the first order, to which the whole universe has given its assent, that the greatest crimes which afflict human society are all committed beneath a false pretence of justice. The greatest of all crimes, at least that which is the most destructive, and consequently the most opposite to the design of nature, is war; but there is not a single aggressor, who does not gloss over his guilt with the pretext of justice....

I believe, then, that the ideas of just and unjust are as clear and universal as the ideas of health and sickness, truth and falsehood ...

The Ignorant Philosopher, Section xxxii (1766).

41   *Justice for all*

One of the great social advances of the *philosophes* lay in their belief that liberty and justice were rights which belonged to all men, and not merely to a privileged group of rulers and aristocrats. The *philosophes* were not so unanimous in their views on equality, which was not generally favoured until the last decades of the century. Voltaire certainly did not believe in the equality of all men, but his belief in the universal principle of justice is one of the noblest inspirations of his age.

Thus the fundamental law of morality acts with equal force upon all the well-known nations. There are a thousand differences in the interpretations of this law, in a thousand different circumstances; but the basis ever subsists the same, and this basis is the idea of justice and injustice.

The Ignorant Philosopher, Section xxxvi (1766). Cf. 5.

42   *To be just, we must be tolerant*

The practical application of these beliefs involves a denial of fanaticism, an acceptance of other people's rights, an active and benevolent tolerance. This is the expression of the command 'adore heaven, and be just'.

A Prayer to God

I address myself, therefore, no longer to men, but unto thee, O God, the Creator of all beings, all worlds, and all ages; if it be permitted such feeble creatures, lost in the immensity of space, and imperceptible to the rest of the universe, to ask any thing of thee, who hast given all, of thee, whose decrees are immutable as they are eternal. Deign to look down in pity on those errors which are inseparable from our nature; and let them not prove our misfortunes! Thou hast not given us hearts to hate, nor hands to destroy each other : Grant that we may mutually assist one another to support the burthen of a painful and transitory life. Let not the trifling difference between the vestments that cover our weak bodies, between our defective languages, our ridiculous customs, our numerous imperfect laws, our idle opinions, our several conditions, so disproportionate in our eyes, and so equal in thine; let not the little shades of rank or party, which distinguish the several atoms called men, be the signals of hatred and persecution! May those who celebrate thy name by wax-light at noon-day, tolerate such as are content with the light of the sun. Let not those who put on a white linen surplice to tell us we must love thee, hold in detestation such as preach the same doctrine in a cloak of black woollen. May it be the same thing to adore thee in a jargon taken from an ancient language, as in a similar jargon formed on a modern one. May those whose garments are dyed red or purple, who domineer over a small part of a little heap of this earth, who possess a few round pieces of a certain shining metal, enjoy without vanity what they call riches and grandeur. May others behold them without envy; for nothing is there in such vanities, thou knowest, to be envied; nothing is there in such grandeur of which to be vain. May all mankind remember that they are brethren; may they hold the tyranny of the mind in abhorrence, and execrate the violence that robs industry of the fruits of its labour. If war be sometimes necessary, let us not destroy each other in the midst of peace; but employ our transitory existence in praising, even from Siam to California, in all the different languages of the earth, thy goodness, to which we are indebted for the present moment of that existence.

A Treatise on Religious Toleration, Ch. xxiii (1763).
Cf. 2.

The following chapter describes the practical ways in which Voltaire endeavoured to achieve this toleration for his fellow men.

Champion of the oppressed

'But we must get you cured.' *Candide*, Ch. iv.
'But we must cultivate our garden.' *Candide*, Ch. xxx.

In his novel *Rameau's Nephew* Diderot at one point contrasted the achievements of the man of letters with those of the man of action, and saw both triumphantly present in the life of Voltaire. Diderot writes 'I would give everything I possess to have done one particular deed. Certainly *Mahomet* [a famous play by Voltaire] is a sublime work to have written, but I would prefer even more to have vindicated the memory of the Calas family.'

Voltaire himself claimed to have more pride in the people calling him 'l'homme aux Calas' ('the man who helped the Calas family') than in all his literary glory.

Throughout his long life he attacked abuses and mocked hypocrisy, but at first these attacks seem to be made from a distance, as if Voltaire were looking in through a window at the follies of the world, and saying 'how ridiculous they are', without himself feeling obliged to *help* those who were suffering. Gradually, though, while his mockery continues, his sympathies for the sufferers are involved, and he seems to say more and more decisively that we should *act*, by helping as best we can.

His attitude is built up both from abstract convictions—his passion for liberty and justice (see chapters on 'England' and 'The *philosophe*')—and from his personal acquaintance with the realities of evil, of pain, of suffering, realities which cannot be argued away or ignored, but which must be faced, and which we must try to overcome. Many examples of his campaigns to help could be given—this chapter gives brief comment on the most famous. Sometimes, as with the Calas affair (47), his efforts met with success, and sometimes, as with the case of the peasants in serfdom to the abbey of Saint-Claude, or the case of La Barre (49), his efforts, though publicizing the injustice, failed to achieve clear positive results. In all of them, however, we see the same striving to act, to *help*.

43   *Suffering is real—whatever the philosophers say*

At the simplest level Voltaire was appalled by those who turn a blind eye to the real horrors of the world, and excuse their inactivity by saying 'Oh, it's all right really, it's just that you don't understand all the circumstances'. Life, Voltaire claimed, proves this attitude all too painfully wrong. Here, Voltaire is being 'shown the world' by two such unworldly philosophers:

They made some very curious distinctions, incessantly assuring me, without knowing what they said, that this world is the best of all really possible worlds. But being just then tortured with the stone, which gave me the most insupportable pain, the citizens of the best of worlds conducted me to the neighbouring hospital. In the way, two of these perfectly happy inhabitants were carried off by two creatures of their own likeness: they were loaded with irons, the one for debt, the other upon mere suspicion. I know not whether I was conducted into one of the best possible hospitals; but I was crowded amongst two or three thousand wretches like myself. Here were several defenders

of their country, who informed me, that they had been tre-
panned and dissected alive; that they had had arms and
legs cut off; and that many thousands of their generous fel-
low-countrymen had been massacred in one of the thirty
battles fought in the last war, which is about the hundred
thousandth war since we have been acquainted with wars.
... After a very sharp iron had been thrust into my
bladder, and some stones extracted from this quarry; when
I was cured, and I had no further complaints, than a few
disagreeable pains for the rest of my days, I made my
representations to my guides. I took the liberty of telling
them there was some good in this world, as the surgeons
had extracted four flints from the centre of my torn in-
trails; but that I would much rather that bladders had been
lanthorns than quarries. I spoke to them of the innumer-
able calamities and crimes that were dispersed over this
excellent world. The boldest of the two, who was a German,
and my countryman, told me, that all this was a mere
trifle.

> *The Ignorant Philosopher*, Section xxvi (1766).
> Cf. 9, 19, 20.

44 So we must do something positive about it

Voltaire says this many times, in terms which echo the
lapidary conclusion of *Candide*. Man's duty is to act posi-
tively—he must love God, and do good. In the 'Gardener's
Catechism' (*Philosophical Dictionary*, 1765) the main character claims, 'I love God with all my heart, and I sell my
vegetables at a very reasonable price.' When he is asked,
'What are your principles?' he answers, 'Why, to be a good
husband, for example, a good father, good neighbour, good
subject and good gardener; I don't aim any higher. and I
trust God will have mercy on me.'

The private citizen must act within the modest limits of
his powers. But the king must do good on a large scale. In
the 'Chinese Catechism' (1764) the prince who will one
day be king is told 'It is not enough for you to do no evil,

you must do good; you will feed the poor, by employing them on useful works, and not by rewarding idleness; you will beautify the highways; you will dig canals; you will raise public buildings; you will encourage all the arts, you will reward merit of every kind; you will pardon involuntary crimes.' (Cf. 34)

45   *Voltaire's example*

Between the humble gardener and the exalted king there is plenty of scope, and Voltaire, finding himself somewhere in between the two, was not idle. Admiral John Byng was condemned to death on 27 January 1757 for 'neglect of duty', having broken off an engagement with the French fleet off Minorca the year before. Voltaire wrote passionate letters of appeal, asking for Byng to be pardoned. The letter that follows (in Voltaire's own English) was sent on 2 January 1757 to Byng, to let him know the favourable support which Richelieu had given to his case.

Sir,
   Tho' I am almost unknown to you, I think 'tis my duty to send you the copy of the Letter which I have just received from the Marshal Duke of Richelieu. Honour, Humanity, and Equity, order me to convey it into your hands. This noble and unexpected Testimony from one of the most candid as the most generous of my countrymen makes me presume y^r Judges will do you the same justice.
   I am with respect,
      Sir
         Y^r most humble ob^t serv^t
            VOLTAIRE

46 *Failure*

Voltaire's appeal, and those of many other people, had no success. Byng was executed on 14 March 1757, and his death is commemorated in one of the most biting passages of *Candide* (Ch. xxiii):

Candide then asked, who was that lusty man, who had been killed with so much ceremony? He received for answer, that it was an Admiral. 'And, pray, why do you put your Admiral to death?—Because he did not kill men enough himself. You must know, he had an engagement with a French Admiral, and it has been proved against him, that he was not near enough to his antagonist.—But surely then, replied Candide, the French Admiral must have been as far from him.—There is no doubt of that, said the other; but in this country it is proper, now and then, to put one Admiral to death, in order to encourage the rest.'

47 *The fight is on: the Calas affair*

Jean Calas, a Huguenot, was tortured and then executed in 1762 for having supposedly murdered his own son. The son had been found dead, and it was thought by the authorities that Calas had killed him to prevent him from turning Catholic. At first, Voltaire thought Calas was guilty, and a fanatic. He wrote to a friend on 22 March 1762:

Perhaps you have heard of a good Huguenot who has been broken on the wheel by the Parlement of Toulouse for having strangled his son. This saintly Protestant even thought that his action was good, since his son wanted to turn Catholic, and this averted an apostasy; he had sacrificed his son to the Lord, and thought himself far superior to Abraham, for Abraham did no more than obey, while our Calvinist hanged his son of his own accord, to keep his own conscience clear. We may not be worth very much, but the Huguenots are worse than us ...

Almost at once Voltaire was doubtful if this was the full story. He wrote for detailed information on 25 March 1762 :

This interests me as a man, and even a little as a *philosophe*. I want to know on which side the horror of fanaticism lies. The Intendant for Languedoc is in Paris. I beg of you, speak to him or get him to speak. He knows the details of this fearsome affair. Be so kind, I pray you, as to let me know what I should think of it all. What an abominable age this is : Calas, Malagrida, Damiens, the loss of all our colonies, notes of confession, and the comic opera.

It is typical that Voltaire should list this affair with other scandals and evils, big or little, of the time.

Voltaire met Calas's widow soon after. He came quickly to believe that Calas was innocent, that he had wrongly been executed for his son's death, and that he and his unhappy family, now persecuted in their turn, must be vindicated. He threw himself into their defence with a fierce, single-minded energy, pouring out a torrent of letters, appeals and pamphlets which led at last and stage by stage to government re-examination of the case. By 1765 the executed father had been recognized as innocent, and some reparation had been made to his family.

Voltaire, and the French public, were not to forget the Calas case. In 1768 Voltaire's *conte*, *The Man of Forty Crowns* summed up the barbaric processes which the family endured :

My memory then represented to me the dreadful fate of the Calas family; a virtuous mother in irons, her children in tears and forced to fly, her house given up to pillage, a respectable father of a family broken with torture, agonising on a wheel, and expiring in the flames; a son loaded with chains, and dragged before the judges, one of whom said to him, '*We have just now broke your father on the wheel, we will break you alive too.*'

48 *Sirven*

The Sirven case, coming soon after, had similarities with the Calas affair. Again, a Protestant family bereaved of one of its children was cruelly persecuted for religious reasons. In *The Man of Forty Crowns* Voltaire follows his résumé of the Calas affair with this account of the Sirvens' misfortunes:

I remembered the family of Sirven, which one of my friends met with among the ice-covered mountains, as they were flying from the persecution of a judge as ignorant as he was unjust. This judge (he told me) had condemned a whole innocent family to death, on a supposition, without the least shadow of proof, that the father and mother, assisted by two of their daughters, had cut the throat of the third, and drowned her besides, for going to Mass. I saw, in judgements of this kind, at once an excess of stupidity, of injustice, and of barbarity.

For the Sirven family Voltaire's campaigning took longer to achieve results, but eventually he achieved some success.

49 *La Barre*

In 1766 a young nobleman of nineteen, the Chevalier de La Barre, was executed at Abbeville. His alleged crime was that of having mutilated a wooden crucifix erected on one of the bridges in the town, and of irreverence and blasphemy before and after this offence. Another nobleman, d'Étallonde, was also condemned, but could not be executed as he had escaped.

Voltaire's anger arose this time from the barbarity of the punishment (cf. 25). The young men may have been guilty —proof was uncertain—but did they deserve such a sentence? Did La Barre deserve to die?

Within a month of La Barre's execution Voltaire had written his pamphlet 'The Account of the Death of the Chevalier de La Barre'. This extract tells most of the gruesome story. The atrocious disproportion between the crime and the punishment was to shock Voltaire into a decade of propaganda, urging the reform of criminal law.

I will tell you more, Sir; in France there is no law expressly condemning one to death for blasphemy. The ordonnance of 1666 prescribes a fine for the first offence, doubled for the second, &c., and the pillory for the sixth repeated offence.

In spite of this the judges of Abbeville, with unbelievable ignorance and cruelty, condemned young d'Étallonde, at eighteen years of age:

1° To suffer the agony of amputation of the tongue at the very root, which is so executed that if the patient does not offer his tongue, it is gripped with iron pincers, and then torn from his throat.

2° To have his right hand severed, before the door of the chief church of the town.

3° Next to be driven in a tumbril to the market-square, there to be fastened to a stake by an iron chain, and to be burnt on a slow fire. The sieur d'Étallonde had happily spared his judges the horror of this execution, by escaping.

Since the chevalier de La Barre was in their hands they had the humanity to soften his sentence, by commanding that he should be beheaded before being cast into the flames; but though they diminished the agony in this respect they increased it in another, by condemning him to suffer both ordinary and extraordinary torture, in order to make him declare who were his accomplices; as if a young man's extravagant behaviour, foolish words of which no trace remains, were a crime against the state, or a conspiracy. This shocking sentence was passed on the 28th February of the present year of 1766.

[An appeal to the Parlement of Paris was unsuccessful, being rejected by fifteen to ten votes on 4 June 1766.]

All France looked on this judgement with horror. The chevalier de La Barre was sent back to Abbeville, to be executed there. The guards who escorted him had to take side-roads, as it was feared that the chevalier de La Barre might be set free on the way by his friends; but this should rather have been hoped for than feared.

At last, on the 1st July of this year, this too memorable execution took place in Abbeville: this youth was first put to the torture. Observe the nature of his torment.

The victim's legs are clamped between planks; iron or wooden wedges are forced between the planks and his knees, so that the bones are smashed. The chevalier fainted, but he soon recovered his senses with the help of spirituous liquors, and declared without complaining that he had no accomplices.

As confessor and helper he was given a Dominican, the friend of his aunt the abbess, and with whom he had often supped in the convent. This good man wept, and the chevalier consoled him. They were served dinner. The Dominican could not eat. 'Let us eat a little food, said the chevalier to him; you will need as much strength as I shall to endure the spectacle which I shall provide.'

The spectacle was indeed terrible: five executioners had been sent from Paris for this execution. I cannot truly say whether his tongue and his hand were severed. All that I know from his letters sent me from Abbeville, is that he climbed the scaffold with a calm and uncomplaining courage, without anger, and without ostentation: all that he said to the monk who was with him can be condensed to these words: 'I had not thought a gentleman would be put to death for so small an offence.'

'For so small an offence.' Voltaire opened France's eyes to the cruelties within its system, to the humbug, fanaticism and complacency which lived on in French society. From age to age these evils recur, and Voltaire's example can help us fight them in our turn.

Select bibliography

1 Works by Voltaire in English translation

Although the eighteenth-century translations of Voltaire have a special interest and attraction, they can rarely be found outside the larger libraries. Some of the more modern translations are listed below.

The Works of Voltaire, 43 vols (New York, 1901-3). This large and fairly complete edition may still be found in many libraries.

The Age of Louis XIV, tr. M. P. Pollack (Everyman's Library: London, 1958).

Candide, available in many editions, e.g.:

   Candide, tr. L. Blair (Bantam Books: New York, 1959).

   Candide, tr. J. Butt (Penguin Books: London, n.d.).

Candide and Other Tales (Everyman's Library: London, 1955).

Philosophical Dictionary, selected and tr. W. Baskin (London, 1962).

Philosophical Dictionary, selected and tr. H. I. Woolf (London, 1945).

The Princess of Babylon (New English Library: London, 1969).

2   Works by Voltaire in French

Œuvres complètes de Voltaire, ed. L. Moland, 52 vols (Paris, 1877-85).

A new complete edition of Voltaire's works is now being published under the direction of Dr Theodore Besterman.

Voltaire's Correspondence, ed. Th. Besterman, 107 vols (Geneva, 1953-65).
Mélanges, ed. J. van den Heuvel (La Pléïade: Paris, 1961).
Œuvres historiques, ed. R. Pomeau (La Pléïade: Paris, 1962).
Romans et contes, ed. H. Bénac (Classiques Garnier: Paris, 1960).
Candide, ed. C. Thacker (Droz: Geneva, 1968).
Dialogues philosophiques, ed. R. Naves (Classiques Garnier: Paris, 1966).
Dictionnaire philosophique, ed. J. Benda and R. Naves (Classiques Garnier: Paris, 1961).
Essai sur les mœurs, ed. R. Pomeau, 2 vols (Classiques Garnier: Paris, 1963).
Lettres philosophiques, ed. F. A. Taylor (Blackwell: Oxford, 1961).
Mémoires pour servir à la vie de M. de Voltaire, ed. J. Brenner (Paris, 1964).

3   Works about Voltaire and his writings

BARBER, W. H., *Voltaire: Candide* (London, 1960). Short, lucid and admirable study of the *conte*.
BESTERMAN, TH., *Voltaire* (London, 1969). The best biography of Voltaire, full, detailed, balanced, excellently written.

KOTTA, N., *L'Homme aux quarante écus: a Study of Voltairian Themes* (The Hague, 1966). The best short study of Voltaire's principal interests.

POMEAU, R., *La Religion de Voltaire* (Paris, 1956).

—— *Voltaire par lui-même* (Paris, 1964).

The series of *Studies on Voltaire and the Eighteenth Century* (Geneva, 1955-) contains many articles and studies of interest concerning Voltaire and his works.